The Nantucket Sea Monster: A Fake
News Story
by Darcy Pattison
Illustrated by Peter Willis
© 2017 Mims House.
All Rights Reserved.

Mims House
1309 Broadway
Little Rock, AR 72202
MimsHouse.com

Publisher's Cataloging-in-Publication data
Names: Pattison, Darcy, author.
Title: The Nantucket sea monster :
a fake news story / by Darcy Pattison.

Description: Little Rock, AR: Mims
House, 2017.
Identifiers: ISBN 978-1-62944-082-8
(Hardcover) | 978-1-62944-083-5 (pbk.) |
978-1-62944-084-2 (ebook) | LCCN
2017904671
Summary: In August 1937 the local paper reported that a sea monster had been spotted
near Nantucket, illuminating both the importance and cost of a free press.
Subjects: LCSH Hoaxes--Juvenile literature. | Freedom of the press--United
States--Juvenile literature. | Impostors and imposture--Juvenile literature. | Decep-
tion--Juvenile literature. | Hoaxes--History--20th century--Juvenile literature. |
Nantucket Island (Mass.)--History--20th century—Juvenile literature. |
BISAC JUVENILE NONFICTION / History / United States / State & Local |
JUVENILE NONFICTION / Social Science / Politics & Government
Classification: LCC Z658.U5 P38 2017 | DDC 363.31/0973--dc23

Nantucket Sound

BILL'S BOAT

Tuckernuck Island

AUGUST 7, 1937 WAS A WARM SATURDAY ON NANTUCKET ISLAND, JUST OFF THE COAST OF CAPE COD, MASSACHUSETTS.

Coatue Beach

Squam Pond

South Beach

Mandaket Beach

Nantucket Island

Across the island, people opened the weekly edition of *The Inquirer and Mirror* newspaper and spread it out. There, in the middle of the front page, was a startling headline:

A SEA MONSTER
BILL MANVILLE SAYS HE SAW ONE OFF NANTUCKET. INSISTS HE WAS NOT DREAMING. HOPES IT APPEARS AGAIN TO VERIFY HIS STORY.

BILL'S BOAT

People read the incredible story from fisherman Bill Manville.

On Wednesday August 4, he'd been out in his boat looking for bluefish, as it was about the time they showed up. After hours with no luck, he discovered the reason for the missing fish.

He saw a terrible looking head rise 15-20 feet above the water.

"It wasn't a whale," he insisted. "I saw the thing with my own eyes about 9:30 this morning."

THE NEWSPAPER STORY ENDED:
"NOW WE ARE WAITING TO HEAR FROM SOMEONE ELSE WHO SAW IT."

Someone else had seen the sea monster. Businessman and sportsman Ed Crocker wrote a letter to the newspaper. He said that on August 4, the same day as Bill Manville, he saw the denizen of the deep.

On Monday, August 9, Gilbert "Gibby" Manter was also looking for bluefish. Instead, a flock of gulls flew overhead acting like they were frightened. And then, he saw it just outside the breaker waves, closer to the tiny Tuckernuck Island than to Nantucket.

"I'VE NEVER SEEN ANYTHING LIKE IT."

The sea monster's head was ugly, with something looking like horns. A light streak ran along its dark greenish side. The back humped out of the water.

"Do you think it was the same thing that Manville saw?" asked the newspaper editor.

"I guess t'was the same creature all right," Gibby said.

The story was gaining credibility. After all, the newspaper printed the stories, so it had to be true. More and more people believed the impossible: a sea monster was hovering around their island. And they were scared.

Ed and Gibby decided to investigate together. On Tuesday, August 10, they were walking along Mandaket Beach when they found something incredible.

FOOTPRINTS!

Excited, they called the newspaper, who sent photographers. The footprints appeared to be from a web-footed animal. They measured about 66" long by 45" wide.

A second set of footprints was reported near Smith's Point and was soon photographed. It was reported that these were the first photographs ever made of a sea monster's tracks.

The newspaper editor telegraphed scientists in Boston and New York for help in identifying the monster: "Can send picture for inspection if desired."

IF THE FOOTPRINTS WERE THAT BIG,

HOW BIG WAS THE MONSTER ITSELF?

Later on August 10, the word spread as friends talked to friends: The sea monster had been captured!

PEOPLE FLOODED THE DOCKS TO SEE IT.

IT'S A KILLER!

JUST A WHALE!

Captain Balfour Yerxa came in. Instead of the sea monster, he had caught three big sand sharks. The sea monster was still out there. Somewhere.

Everyone had something to say about the sea monster.

Dewey Sandsbury said, "That fellow came ashore on the east end of the island last night and drank Squam Pond dry."

Another said that the tracks were so deep that a Coast Guard tractor had to pull Lester Simmon's car out of the sea monster's tracks and onto a firm foundation.

Across the nation, people read of the Nantucket sea monster and shivered.

Meanwhile, Bill Manville asked the Massachusetts Head Fish and Game Warden for information.

138

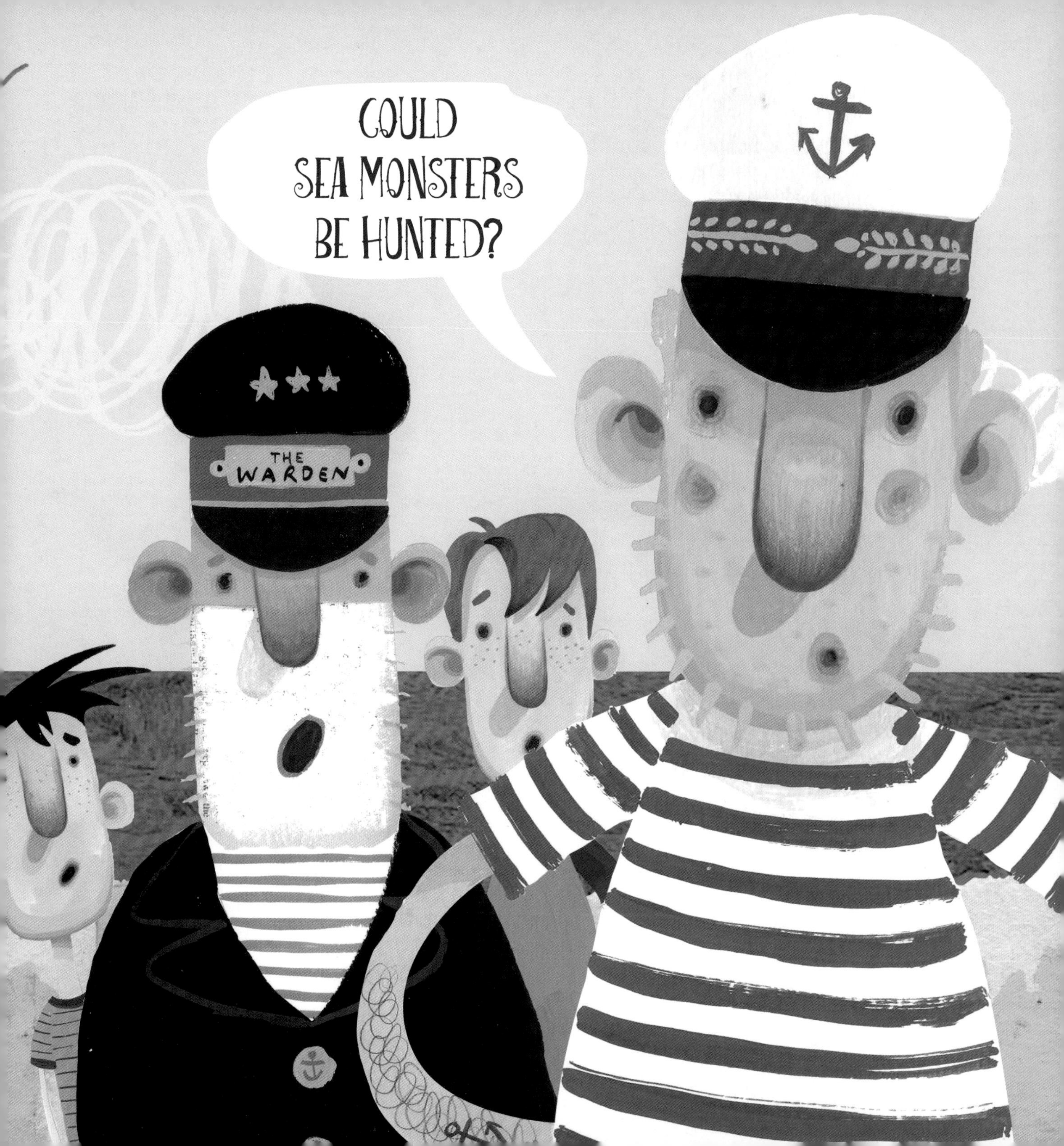
COULD SEA MONSTERS BE HUNTED?
THE WARDEN

On Saturday, August 14, the weekly paper printed eyewitness stories and photographs of the sea monster tracks. Scientists at the Harvard Museum of Zoology and the Boston Aquarium studied the footprint photos and reported back. They both said that they didn't know any creature capable of making such tracks.

But then, all seemed quiet.

WHEN THEY GOT THERE,

Suddenly, on Wednesday, August 18, news came: Tony Sarg had caught the sea monster. It was dragged up onto the South Beach.

Everyone ran to the beach. Maybe it was just sand sharks again, but they had to see.

THEY COULDN'T BELIEVE THEIR EYES.

The sea monster was a huge rubber balloon.

It was made by Tony Sarg, the famous puppeteer and owner of the local Curiosity Shop. Since 1928, he had designed the massive balloons that flew over the Macy's Thanksgiving Day Parade.

The 135-foot sea monster was one of Sarg's balloons. The whole thing had all been a big publicity stunt.

The August 21 issue of *The Inquirer and Mirror* explained the elaborate hoax. Sarg, along with Macy's officials, decided to put on a publicity stunt. They would float the balloon near a beach and create a stir. They talked with the newspaper's editor and other newsmen on the island and off the island. All the newsmen agreed to go along. Perthe News, which created newsreels, sent cameramen on August 16 to film the sea monster.

The newspaper said, "As a result Nantucket was mentioned in favorable news stories from Cape Cod to California. The actual cash value of the space obtained is difficult to estimate but will run into many thousand of dollars."

R.H. Macy and Company of New York City, the newspaper said, did not attempt to commercialize, or make money, from the event. They were only mentioned because Mr. Sarg had created their balloons. The newspaper story concluded:

"TO DATE NO ONE HAS REPORTED SUFFERING FROM THE RESULTS OF THIS PUBLICITY STUNT."

THE NANTUCKET SEA MONSTER FLEW
IN THE 1937 MACY'S THANKSGIVING DAY
PARADE AND WAS SEEN BY MILLIONS.

TIMELINE OF ACTUAL EVENTS

1936 or 1937. Tony Sarg designed a sea monster balloon for the Macy's Thanksgiving Day Parade. He went to the Goodyear Tire and Rubber Company in Akron, OH to discuss the sea monster balloon.

Early 1937. Staff of R. H. Macy and Company in New York City and Sarg discussed publicity for the 1937 parade. Someone suggested a sea monster sighting. They decided on Nantucket because Sarg had a store and a home there, and Macy's founder was from Nantucket.

March 13, 1937. Nantucket Publicity Committee established, Gibby Manter, Chairman.

Before August 1937. Sarg discussed the plan with the prominent business men of Nantucket and the editor of *The Inquirer and Mirror.* All agreed with the plan.

Before August 1937. The sea monster plan was discussed with newspapermen both on and off the island. All agreed with the plan.

Before August 1937. Sarg arranged for the sea monster balloon to be shipped from Akron, OH to Nantucket Island first by train, and then by ship.

Wednesday, August 4, 1937. Bill Manville reported that he saw a sea monster. Ed Crocker later said he saw a sea monster that same day.

Saturday, August 7, 1937. *The Inquirer and Mirror* published the first report of the sea monster.

Monday, August 9, 1937. Gibby Manter claimed that he saw the sea monster.

August 9 or 10, 1937. Someone made sea monster footprints in the sand.

Tuesday, August 10, 1937. Footprints of the sea monster were found and photographed.

Tuesday, August 10, 1937. Captain Balfour Yerxa brought in three large sand sharks.

Saturday, August 14, 1937. *The Inquirer and Mirror* published several more articles about the sea monster.

Sometime between August 14 and August 18, 1937. The 300-pound sea monster balloon arrived at the Railway Expressway Agency offices on Nantucket Island, along with 9000 pounds of compressed gas cylinders.

Wednesday, August 18, 1937. The sea monster balloon was inflated on the remote Coatue Beach on the north side of the Nantucket Harbor. It was floated across the harbor toward the city and wound up at the South Beach.

Thursday, August 19, 1937. The balloon was re-inflated so islanders could see it again. Tony Sarg joined the group and played with the children. Many people took photos which wound up in family photo albums.

Saturday, August 21, 1937. *The Inquirer and Mirror* wrote an article explaining the sea monster stunt. The story was signed by the editor and seven men: O.D. Ingall, Charles E. Congdon, Fred D. Bennett, Finest S. MacLaughlin, William D. Thomson, Leslie Martin, Sidney W. Thurston, Isaac Hills. William L. Mather and the editor H. B. Turner. All but three men—Congdon, Thomson, and Turner—were members of the 1937 Nantucket Publicity Committee.

Thursday, November 26, 1937. The Nantucket Sea Monster balloon flew over New York City as part of the Macy's Thanksgiving Day Parade. It was the only year this balloon flew in the parade.

A FREE PRESS AND THE FAKE NEWS

Freedom of the press is guaranteed in the First Amendment of the U.S. Constitution. From the beginnings of the United States, statesmen understood that a free press was important. Reporters could study and report about what the government was doing. It means that politicians can't do whatever they want because they might get caught. Instead, they must follow the law like everyone else. Thomas Jefferson, the 3rd U.S. President and the author of the Declaration of Independence put it like this:

"Where the press is free, and every man able to read, all is safe."[1]

However, when the press is free to print what it likes, sometimes it will print things that are false. Some laws make sure the press doesn't write slander. Slander means you write a lie about someone. Otherwise, newspapers can print what they like. Thomas Jefferson also wrote:

"Nothing can now be believed which is seen in a newspaper."[2]

From the beginning of the United States, free press has printed both truth and lies. When things are working right, there's more truth than lies. Sometimes, though, like in the story of the Nantucket sea monster, editors will deliberately print something false. At the time, the editor said the articles were fine because 1) no one was hurt, and 2) Macy's company didn't commercialize, or try to make money, from the event. However, they freely admit that the publicity for Nantucket Island was worth thousands of dollars.

Was the publicity stunt right or wrong?

❧ VOCABULARY ❧

Hoax - An event planned to fool people.

Publicity - Being mentioned a lot in the news media. The media could be newspaper, radio, television, or online.

Publicity stunt - An event planned to get public attention for marketing purposes.

Credibility - A story or statement that is believable or trustworthy.

Free press - The First Amendment of the U.S. Constitution says that Congress can't pass laws that limit what a newspaper can write. This guarantees a "free press." In other words, newspapers are free to investigate and write about whatever stories they want.

Slander - Writing a lie about a person.

❧ SOURCES ❧

All quotes are taken directly from newspaper accounts in Nantucket's *The Mirror and Inquirer* newspaper, which is available online at the Nantucket Atheneum's Digital Historic Newspaper Archive: http://bit.ly/NantucketNewspaper

1) "Thomas Jefferson to Charles Yancey, 6 January 1816," Founders Online, National Archives, last modified March 30, 2017, http://founders.archives.gov/documents/Jefferson/03-09-02-0209.

2) "Thomas Jefferson to John Norvell, 11 June 1807," Founders Online, National Archives, last modified March 30, 2017, http://founders.archives.gov/documents/Jefferson/99-01-02-5737.